A GATHERING OF MOTHER TONGUES

D1546279

A GATHERING OF MOTHER TONGUES

POEMS BY
JACQUELINE JOHNSON

6/3/98

For Jacqui,

my name sake.

At least this is
finished faster
than my quilts! :-)

Enjy!

Jackie

WHITE PINE PRESS · FREDONIA, NEW YORK

Acknowledgments:
I would like to acknowledge the support and help of the following people and organizations: Marie Brown for believing always...; the New Renaissance Writers Guild, John O. Killens Writers Workshop, Our Book Own Fair, PEN Writers Association, Authors Guild, Robert Rauschenberg Foundation, New York Foundation for the Arts, Mid-Atlantic Writers Association, MacDowell Colony for the Arts, the Frederick Douglass Creative Arts Center, Blue Mountain Center, the Jenkins and Johnson Clans, Gloria Johnson and Pat Johnson—indelibly sisters forever—and Louise Merriwether for always being a bright light on my path. A thousand thanks to Maurice Kenny, Dennis Maloney, Elaine LaMattina, Bree Bishop, and Betty LaDuke. Thanks Priscilla Milligan, Candis Sanders, Ted Lawton, Janet Griffiths, Marolla Griffiths, Anne Bailey, Sharon Dupree, Pat Warrington, Anne and Charlie Sanders, Julie Broglin, Randy Williams, Catherine McKinley, Judith Baumel, Daniel Garrett, Leslie Holmes, and my Kiamsha sisters for listening, nurturing and putting up with me. To the most high!

The cover art is a two-color reproduction of Betty LaDuke's acrylic painting *Africa: Market Day Dreams*. Copyright ©1997 by Betty LaDuke. Used by gracious permission of the artist.

Book Design: Elaine LaMattina
Author Photograph: Ted Lawton

Printed and bound in the United States of America
ISBN 1-877727-79-2

Published by
White Pine Press, 10 Village Square, Fredonia, New York 14063

Library of Congress Cataloging-in-Publication Data
Johnson, Jacqueline, 1957–
        A gathering of mother tongues : poems / by Jacqueline Johnson.
        p.   cm.
        "1997 White Pine Press poetry prize winner."
        ISBN 1-877727-79-2 (alk. paper)
        I. Title.
PS3560.037884G3   1998
811.54—dc21   98–12879
                                                             CIP

In the memory of Henrietta Jenkins and Joseph Johnson,
my mother and father tongue.
May the sweet wine of life come again.

For Etta,
my first words, source of my true mother tongue.

A GATHERING OF MOTHER TONGUES

A Knowing

Notes on the Poems

A GATHERING OF MOTHER TONGUES

BIRTH OF MY ORIGINS

Mama,
it is with a thief's luck
I now wear your face.
Some days, are spent floundering
on a shore of girl-women,
where I have neither a home
nor solace of my woman wisdom.

All my life, I have been looking for you,
your laughter and your arms.
Mother of rebel heart, fire-speaker,
my first song. All my life I have looked for you
and found so many lacking. Here in
this black urban village are
women holding little pieces
of earth trying to believe
it is the whole world.
I am aware this lie is jest,
a half-filled calabash of being
niece, stepchild, godchild, grandchild,
deeta though never daughter.
I am always hungry,
aching to claim my own sea,
my own forever.

All my life, I have been painting
the same picture. Cerulean blue of the ocean,
mauve colored clouds of early morning,
granules of sand on my feet,
blaring seacoast white of the sun,
rising holy, singular. Again
and again, I return to this shore seeking,
questioning, how many women?

How many women, lord,
does it take to find you mama?
A waterfall of mother tongues
fills my ears. I squat,
prepare to birth myself.

What is there for us
five generations deep,
we daughters of the dark, open
sinew of our people,
search our mother's truths
for our own things.
Calabash of ancient secrets
eludes us.

What dumb luck some
daughters have.
Like a village bride
on her wedding night,
we surrender everything,
only to wake up and peer into
some narrow mouth calabash,
our mothers, our grandmothers
call our wealth.
Oh, it is the same one
their mothers passed to them.

Mother carried calabash
of her dreams, silvered,
brilliant on her tongue.
Her hands ammonia reddened,
worked sunup to sundown struggling
to fill that widening, bottomless
bowl, never knowing wicked
satiation of dreams fulfilled.

Even now, we daughters know
a great nothing.
What to do with this rage,

centuries old, stubborn
as naps in the nape of my neck.
We circumference the edge
and beginning of a universe
only we have the keys to.

Some of us know well how to meet
those same women on the road,
holding what knives and sticks we can.
We strip ourselves of all obvious wealth,
hoping to protect our womenselves
from their envy,
age long desire to see us broken,
like the milkless,
flabby tits of a grandma. These women,
bitter and hard veined believe,
believe, the world is as
small as their vision.

I never expected to bury
new shoots of so many unfurled dreams,
to fight for breath, meaning amongst my sisters,
women who wear my own skin.
I gather courage, and walk
the winding path between
girl and woman. I claim, savor
sweet salt of my woman waves.
I speak in mother tongues, languages,
they don't know here. Just the same,
I scratch the earth for my meaning.

What there is for us,
we daughters wrestle from our mothers' tongues

singing our own songs,
carrying faith larger than that empty bowl,
our vision as wide as this earth,
love stronger than death.
We, who are the calabash and
its contents,
we, the reshaped, renewed clay
know, today,
today is our own!

I was baptized by
field holler, Bessie wail
caught in the silver of my throat.
At the center of my house in Philadelphia
where the bullets crossed,
was music, ancient,
down home,
sanctified jazz.

(For SJ)

I believe you came
right out of the stars.
Skin the color of eggplant,
caribe two braids covered your head.
It was always something to watch
your healers hands turn a piece of
scrap cloth into a broken slave chain,
wedding band, strip quilt. You patched
uneven squares of your mother's thunder,
transformed yourself into an
elegant african broadcloth, becoming fertile,
healing, like an akuabna dancing
around a slender waist in wind.

I remember you worked three jobs,
two that should have gone to men.
When you gave your baby back,
some of the light went out of you, though
you had a seer's eye. Seeing auras around
plants and babies, talking about times
twenty years from now. It must've been
a struggle to be around regular folks.
You took those nobody-wants-you children,
enduring bites, tantrum kicks to get one word
of understanding, of knowingness out of them.
More than queen bee, diva or high priestess,
you wore earth shoes, chewing a licorice stick,
talking long yin about cleansing, healing our
body, our minds. Put the tongue of understanding
on all of us. We black-eye-susans blossoming,
coming delta strong. Your spirit, a
precious medallion around our lives.

(for Audre Lorde)

A Tryptch—Part I

*"There was never a thing about beingg alive
and sing and not sing."*
                                    —Bernice Reagan

I don't know when it happened or why, she just stop singing. Seem like her voice was too much to hold in the air. She walked around afraid of her own sound, the heart-thumping truth of her life. Most days her life meant struggle, eat, work and more struggle.

She stopped singing afraid of those high notes she used to wrap her love in and send flying over us free, like sun in the morning. Every once in a while she would sing a low note or two, struggling against the grain of her fears, but they were tentative and always searching for a fuller range. She had a whole orchestra in her throat, she knew that and still she conjured up silence. She lived with the agony of a mute, unable to gather her thoughts and give them life, unable to release her sounds in the air, trusting it to carry her. Her auralight went and so did her belief. She thought she had lost her waters, had lost her possibilities.

She had never been told that her voice, her woman sounds, heart sounds, wombsong, foot notes were necessary and sacred as wild thunder raining between brown thighs. She had grown tired of having to apologize for her life, of having to justify her breathing. It was alright, there was enough air for her too? Strangers, friends, lovers always wanting her strength, craving her beauty, that intangible something she didn't even name yet. They were always trying to grasp at her soulmeat and have a free eat, leave her the dirty wrappers from their own lives. They would tell her, "we're starving, we need more, why didn't she offer up her life." The broken vessels spouted for years.

She wondered about her sound, would sense storm of her feelings rising. She had stopped singing, not knowing if she ever would again.

One day, wandering through old selves, she tripped and fell over the sores of her dreams. She ate the red dirt she had fallen into. She began to dig into the earth, into herself, the tops of flowers, into the aching sea of her womb. Everywhere she dug, there was music, there were her forgotten songs, some broken with time, silvered beyond song, or so foreign she didn't recognize the sounds. Ancient hoot wail of Mama Rainey surrounded her. August breath of amazon war women haunted and filled her. She heard the wild dahlia of her song, and wove herself into its layers.

Whole lifetimes of pain, years of dreamhurt, deep deep, anger fell from her, cracking soured eggs and all the things she never did and something else, her fear. It was the last thing to leave her.

Whole notes found her tongue, her lips, broke free of her mouth. Oceans, wildseas, coco palms, children, pieces of kente, red cloth, and ancient gris-gris fell from her mouth until all that was left of her was song.

In this time of sounding, listen closely. You can hear her singing sometimes, in red winged dawns of African, free women.

In my village in Bed-Stuy,
we rally strength against day
and night stalkers. In every block
like in Soweto, there are at least
four or five of us, who fight with
pens, paint, nimble fingers through
hair, song and resistance fire.
I look in any direction in my neighborhood,
and know just like in Azania,
there are no hottentots, but there
are women, who fight, raise homes
from the ground, children and dreams.
Late at night or early in the morning,
on a lunch break they are writing, singing song,
painting, weaving new futures into cloth.
What do you think Bessie Head was doing all those
years? Do you know why was Miriam singing so hard?
Who do you think made those beaded bracelets you wear?
All these women artists presumed dead,
and missing in action, create in places
where light may not be visible
but sight is never lost.
In my village like so many others,
no patrilineal anything,
can undo this truth.

It could have been 1929,
but it was 1927 when
Lois Johnson got born
way down in Moultrie,
Georgia. Could you imagine coming
into your womanhood with
touch of red clay under your feet,
inside your shoes. Right from the
get go, this red earth taught you
what giving was, what foundation was.
Can you imagine coming out of a place where
sweet smell of magnolia covered everything.
God's grace was cool buttermilk and biscuits
so light, only you had the touch to deliver them.
Can you see Lois coming, growing into
herwomanself, coming fully into her five foot frame,
looking for a way to be her black self...
Where does a black woman go for
freedom in 1940, in 1950? Where does a
black woman go for freedom?

Oh sweet rose of Zion,
keeper of kindness,
brown lady, Georgia brown lady,
Harlem fashion plate,
Chef of the late-night three course meal.
Owner of the red hair of Georgia Creole.
Good woman from Moultrie.
You, who were your father's light
and your mother's keeper.
Owner of ancient calabash. Auntie,
you were here when the Savory really jumped,
when Ellington was Duke and Adam Clayton Powell Jr.

25

made the call. But more than that,
you were here when we came along.
Ancient queen of the gettchie gummie,
sister of the sit-down women,
a wise maw-maw lady.

Call it pancakes and bacon at
seven o'clock in the morning,
after the party we, daughters
and sons of other mothers filled
up your house, became folks
you couldn't get rid of,
became like family.

Oh, sweet rose of Zion,
keeper of kindness, all the magic you had
could be found inside love.
All the magic you had
was the inside of love.

Oh, sweet rose of Zion,
      fly free,
            fly free.

THE DELTA

For Gerri Wilson

Alabama harmattan calling me.
At the roots of my hair sits the Mississippi,
through seven generations
sweet burning sage of tradition lives.

Over brass rim of Armstrong freedom growl,
under healing rib of black woman cry,
spirit of Erzulie walks freely
admid blackened and cracked stones of confederate dream.
My soul opens,
translucent with pearls of living.
Under Natchez sun sits my fifth eye,
ancient with the wildness of peacock feathers.

Baptism by orange earth scented water
reveals Phumizule, Shreveport singer
wearing golden crown of Oshun.
Oldest mother, freedom fighter, river mistress
could dance a poem around the moon.
All night, all night
she would sing, chirp, poet
cerulean Biloxi blues
thrice seasoned delta moan
found on the pike between
New Orleans and Azania.
Her crown of feathered wisdom
opalescent and gaudy
crashing through nightminds solitude.

With so much love
the delta claims her own.
Phumizule gave back her voice,

gives up her dance, gave
back the moon.

Still, I can feel Alabama wind,
scent of Erzulie, yellow rose of Oshun
running deep at the roots of my hair,
knocking me over with the fullness of living.

Oh owner of wind,
keeper of river mists,
daughter of the nines,
gateway to the past,
power woman, keeper of hurricanes
tornadoes, twisters, wild, wild
wind who is woman.
Raging purple gale force,
song of a million ancestor voices
ancient dervish whirling
wet, weeping, wind whipping
back the rooftop of our minds.
Turning up the earth, calling up
all our old names, to remind us
how we come here, wealthy with
nothing at all, sounding woman
buffalo wail over this urban mesa.
My tongue is swollen with red dirt as she
gathers funky, pitch blackness of
an ancient, African wind wave.
Our history repeats like so many stutters.

Oh wind, who is woman,
furious flapping which
takes no one, she changes lives
forever, reminding us how we come here,
wealthy with nothing at all. Not even
shanty town wall remains
nor stone fortress where your children slaved.
Start again, she whispers, and
she brought along her sister,
a large and silver wave. Remember how you
live here, wealthy, with nothing at all.

She called upon her sister,
a large and silver wave.

Down to the nines, woman that
closes the circle, that ends this century,
blowing away the brick boundaries of our beliefs,
august tree of our stubbornness,
winded madness of our oppression.
There is nothing we can hide
she upturns it all.
Oh wind, who is woman,
a wild and funky force.
Oh wind, who is power woman,
bring us burnt stones
of new beginnings, hope rekindled,
spitfire dreams weaving a time
we have never seen before.
Oh wind, who is woman,
we are down to the nines.

SOUND OF BROKEN WINGS

*"Come celebrate with me
that something has tried
to kill me and failed."*
—Lucille Clifton

> *Underneath the moon,*
> *tiger of gold and shadow*
> *looks down at [her] claws,*
> *unaware that in the dawn*
> *they lacerate a man.*
>
> *—Jorge Luis Borges*

How he tried to steal my words
push back my thunder.
Do you know how many times
this scene repeats, as another woman
like me, lays fighting
legs spread, knife to
her throat, fucking through
her fear, baring her breast
though not her heart. How many
times have I pushed back music
now broken, now blue, back into
root, empty calabash of the years.
How I reach for you and pull
back at the same time. Lovers
dance eclipsed by wounds
that leave no visible scars.
How do I open myself with arms
that will not embrace,
enter eyes that are closed?
How do I heal wounds that do not bleed?

Can you imagine some man wanting
to control my womanspace, tremble
in my vagina, damn the rivers of my need.
Can you see rage of the body,
age of the spirit.
How I hardly speak now and
never laugh. How he tried to take

33

my second mouth, my me music.
This man who hated his mama,
trussels me in his arms,
and I am lonely forever and never
his. How he tries to orchestrate my
coming, obscure the waterfall
underneath my eyes.

More than white blood
of his coming, here
are the soundings of woman
buffalo wail, fighting in my
muddied rivers, shunning reason,
arms of refuge. My second mouth closes.
I am covered by a darkness so vast,
wild geese feed upon dry manna of this moment.
Ancient lover, now mute and bound, in her place
a foaming stripped tiger becomes my totem.

Need greater than reason,
serpentine tongue
slips between my lips
nuzzles then suckles
crazy circles around my fear.
Spotted freckles on our tongues
tell more of our common gift.
Hearts, bodies ripened
chalice for winded
spirits seeking solace.
How do I love you in
my two steps forward eight steps
backward kind of way.
Still, I open myself
as you try to push past all
those fighting dahomey women.
Sounds of wounded tigers bind
me, tearing a pawed anger upon your face.
I lose myself in the endless blues of the sea.
Count the dead horses upon the shore,
find your face among them.

It was the hurt he didn't see
that kept her away from him.
Under folds of her skin,
between cleft of collar bone,
behind silver film of her eyes,
salted rivers of unknown dimension swelled.

Breaking crystal of her voice
above nightsun shattered his peace.
Her music, her scent, half-filled his hunger.
Didn't want to remember how many times
he'd seen her walking
down any street, in any dream.
Her harpooned heart could only make
wailing sounds of a Rainey moan.

Near the wild pulse of her wrists
behind curve of her knee,
translucent beads of her pain gathered.
She stopped counting times she bared
her shoulders, her life
to half interested eyes.
Always picking up the black pearls
hiding them deeper under her skin.

She couldn't walk for the weight
of centuries needing. So he brought
her rain filled loam of his hands,
love strong and seasoned like the bark of oak.
They were each others' lightning.

Somewhere beyond her natural eyes
bloomed flowers of forgiveness.

Wave after wave of her
woman song washed over her
until she lost, then discovered herself
marked and tall with life,
an urgency of her own.

She discovered a place of beauty,
marks of courage, truth in herself,
persistent as babies breath.

She wore the black pearls free,
shimmering in her eyes.

Leothy Owens
Doris Jean Austin

Everyday you were dying
right in front of our faces.
Laughing through your coughing,
labored breathing, as you worked
sixteen hour days with more
energy and joy than most.

It was something to watch
your large African queen body
change and change as your
skin became a wrinkled sack
cloth that covered your soul.

You stand tall preparing for
chemotherapy. You survive
this bloodletting with grace,
wrapping your hairless head
with gelees, funky diva hats
and sometimes you show the bald
perfect shape of your head letting
us see the goddess shining through.
For a moment you are well, hope burns
like kindling warming your days.

One dark, frigid morning in December,
I look up and realize you are gone.
Wizened angel, black as you wanna
be, flying straight right out of here.

Summer days disrupted by trickster's
hand at play. Someone's child, brother,
son dressed all in red fell across
cement of a brownstone stoop.
Bullet casings sprayed over the ground.
One can hardly see the blood on his
clothes except for the outlines of an
unknown country gathering width across
his back. The old men who witness
his fall, stand back, afraid.
Grapevine hurricane of children
talking among themselves rushing
past fear or reason to see the fallen
one. It's almost like going to a party,
this excitement lights their faces.
A block away robust sounds of gospel
music burst through the air like trumpets.
A weird epiphany it's churchtime in the streets
and worshippers stand, arms raised with their
mind on the lord, unaware a child
dies in full view, while they celebrate.

I listen to this
Harjo woman. Creek
Indian. Out of her mouth
come the fish of many tongues.
Ancestor breath, hot
and warning of a time
between worlds. How
do we give birth
inhabit the fifth world?

Memories of a Lakota woman,
murdered but not dead, flow through her.
I spend hours alive with ths red woman's
vision, combing truth from roots of my hair
to the ends of the earth and back again.

As I walk winding dirt path
I take a feather, yellow flowers
as my bounty. Cut my tongue by sounds
of this sacred buffalo woman singing.

See how all those feathers fly, revealing
evening of a cloudless sky.

WHOLING

Everyday we practice warfare,
no matter how simple.
Dishes doing a sudsy battle with stories,
children of my dreams sleeping lazily in
my womb where angers have gathered
dispossessed of reason.
Broad light of my visions struggle
to scale walls of monthly mooncycles.
How do I make generations
on this delicate crossroads to life.
Unfilled needs turning upon themselves
I arm myself and prepare to let go.
Though I am fond of circles,
roundness that repeats.
Empty calabashes beckon me
to fill them, find the gifts underneath them.
Tired, I swallow dried corn husks.
On a knife strewn with my blood,
I watch some of the women I have been
fall away, as I make peace with old selves.
This is something I must do.
The salt of my power depends on this sweetness.
Now and only now can I
scratch the dawn into my skin, until
I bleed new futures.

Trpytch - Part II

I like how you come and sit with me
watching as I stutter in my broken tongue
by a river of a thousand faces
I search, search for one clear
place where I can still see myself, whole.
Urgently, I peel back the fruit of my skin,
listening to those screaming women that live
in me. Who will silence them, make sweet their anger.
Who will taste blackgum gap of my teeth,
damn the pain inside of my womb.
Who will guide my search among this forest
of dahomey women all wearing my face, speaking at
once in tree, swahili and ancient indian tongue.
Inside my heart, I turn and turn
into this woman I call myself. See how I learn
her, crawling with stones under my eyes,
doing dances that shake waist beads near
small curve of my back. She gives me her trust
as I gather courage to open.
Watch how my masks fall away,
that beauty, even scares me.

Listen, these are my soundings.
I open them up,
hoping to make song again.

You must come and hold me again,
pull me into the soft cradle of your voice,
sugar through madnesses magnificent umbrage.
We pick among our thoughts like pigeons.
You break my fall into a ocean
whose current threatens to take me
outside/inside the bottom of an aloneness
where the delta of my womb weeps.
I have paid this water woman
her price. Still, she demands more.
Everything is up for game, why and
how I won't give you what we
both know, you already have.
You fill me up easily
talking about girl, you could...
What I know of these moments
is more like returning from wars
earth broken, unfilled gourd cracking.
I run, not believing you see my sun
enough to ginger it back to me.
Survivals' kiss opening and unfolding
silver layers of sky music.
How I find the day
against the brown, peaceful
earth of your back.

Dungarees and silk,
chicken gravy and grits,
bitter hearts splattered
loosely on virgin snow.

Days open like fresh pomegranates,
  a little at a time
    a little at a time
sweetness of life is revealed.

A brown, arched back
giving way to dance.
Ancestral dreams ginger our steps.

Girl, you got so much yin and yang
in them braids, too healthy for me.

A disconnected connection
a rhythm without time
days in March limbo
dance through my life.
Aprils rain monsooning in March
nature changes the beat.
The earth does a mega cycle
as I sit outside
inside myself.
My eyes have ears and everything
is triple blue.
Still sewing the winters' seeds
I can't tell the act
from the action.
I live in a double reality.
Everything's a mess
and everything is alright.

Over time, very slowly
I learn to give,
to swing and sway with the elements like
lean, white branches of
birch and willow.
I learn to let go,
trusting the earth
to keep me, it is so simple
this wisdom. Yet fears and my
ids surrey about, pulling me
under wet clay, so many masks,
gray dirt of dreams that have not
found the proper food. Already
I have fallen into
open arms of the sky,
as a thousand drops of rain,
fertile sperm for my hungry
selves, feeds me. I know
this giving way is more than
a stripping of bark, clothes,
and old obsessions. Opening of
purple chrysalis, that quickening
one hears as day surrenders to dusk.
This burnished, nighttime sun is all my own.
I savor it, swallowing blue fired
flames whole.

I sit in the living room
that really is the day room
looking at the soft, ancient
faces of strangers,
finding your face among them.
I wonder can we become family again,
cross bridges, splinter thin,
fragile from so much leaning.
You look like 'Re Franklin
out of "Spirit in the Dark" days
wearing one of those never-go-back afros.
In the sixties you joined the sit-ins,
went to war against the system, learned to
dance the fanga and cook big pots of
groundnuts, chicken, coconut and yellow rice.
In the sixties you fell in love with a woman
who carried the Mississippi in her eyes,
wore the scent of wild marigold all over her
captured the laughing buddha in your heart.

Your life, a drum pulse in many lives.
How you carried children of the battered
from one dream to another. You cared,
though saving lives was much harder than
saving souls. Sometimes you did both.
Pulling back sweet baobab tree of your
spirit, whose strength was many lives deep,
didn't mean you could not be broken, just that
you had a lot to teach. Even in your wisdom
you felt wrong, different, tortured by the litany
of others. Sister with the power of seven people,
daughter of the water,
fine edge of raw silk,
our best gold.

When you surrendered your mind
and walked into this house
that you now share with ten others,
we came too, a scattering of mother tongues
shaking the dry earth
becoming pus of many seasons living.

Behind your eyes a healing begins,
laboured like your breathing,
where we cannot reach nor see.
You lean back on the couch,
sucking in grey smoke
relishing the years, reflecting
like diamonds in your eyes.

October everywhere,
brassy sounds of rolling sky.
Desires, dreams
hanging heavy over me.

Leaves sunset browns, honeyed oranges,
lemon glazed yellows,
greet my eye
warm winter burgundies,
florescent evergreens greening.

Wind rustling in trees
gentle, soothing.
My desire is to lay naked
on this multicolored carpet,
slowly letting this delicious afternoon
song rise,
    rise in my body.

Pretty soon it will begin
all over again, earth closing
becoming a silent, unembraceable woman,
wealthy with food to last a season.

New feelings challenge me to answer.
Under cloud cover, leaves drop to a lake.
My reflection surprises me,
another woman stares back,
pressing me to answer her,
to feed her this whole winter through.

Naked trees dance in the midst
like Shiva's many arms,
their branches surrender to wind.
Rain glistens, silvered
by time's twilight.
Trees, flowers grass make bearable
this place, where I live
between brick, broken languages
and the progress myths of
old world people.
They dance, these naked spirit trees,
lusting in wetness that covers them.
Air breaks open, pulsing with
hum of people gathering for dinner,
lovers twilight kiss of youth,
dusky soundings of a midnight muse.
In this misted magic of Spring
my aloneness, my separatness
is washed away.
Yet, I am not lost
but learning the
one sound of the people.
For the first time,
their doors
are open to me.
I am not afraid.

I am dreaming in colors.
It is raining everywhere.
Fat fish flicker across a lake.
Somebody is very pregnant.

Humseeking woman
secrets in her navel
as tight as
hot skin stretched
across a drum
rounded deepness of
calabash is
more her home.
Repository of sound
maker of music
light behind
the scene, beat
before the drum
beating out notes
as light as
gentle riffs of Ellington.
Sifter of melodies,
chordworker,
spiritcatcher,
a righteous sounding
    early,
early in the morning.

SISTER SUKIE

For Tisha Watson

I always loved Peaches of Simone's "Four Women".
Full, rawsilk afro covering
red earth of three continents
deep of women carrying revolution
in their hands, wombs and mouths.
Women so anonymous, so familiar,
so universal in their Africaness
they could be from Haiti, Ghana or Brooklyn.
Disaporan worn, unflinching, they
chew burning coals, keep watch
with hands full of cloth, words and
unknown strength. Some make a
talisman of their lives,
becoming pathways for the lost.
It's how we never stop making life,
never stop loving, how we never
stop healing and giving, giving.
Someone always remembers how, what
and who we are. Rounded surface of my
back where ancient galaxies live, expanding.
Every woman is a door to a new place, gourded
melody of green rain, creations
wonder. Say sister sukie,
where did you get such
a brown, pretty baby?

Moments wash
one into another, like
yellow flutter of fish
fins. My dreams dart and
dash. Some I catch,
some I lose in this elusive
chase. How I smell the change,
insistent rumbling in my head,
fervent shudder in my womb,
blind chaos that passes for my heart.
Sounding of a
cacophony of tongues.
I am undone
by a vast wholeness
I am just knowing...

A FEW GOOD MEN

For John O. Killens

Slavers stole them out of Akebulan
ageless, red skin, berry bark colored, juju men.
Could have been Diop they took
but it was John Henry Clark, might have been
Che, but it was Malcolm X they stole.
They paid for Ngugi wa Thiong'o
but it was John O. Killens they took.
Might have been Nkrumah, though it was
Dubois they chained.

They had stolen what they thought
were sub human beings.
Try as slavers might,
everything the medicine men
touched, changed.
Everywhere they walked,
new ground opened up.
All the words they wrote, they preached
gathered ashe, flowing into
minds and spirits of their people.
Try as slavers might
they could/can not stop,
furious movement of African life
claiming its own.

If he had lived during
the time of U.N.I.A.
he would have been a Garvite, no doubt.
As it is, he is my brother,
champion spirit of struggle,
ebonied son of the trickster.
He carries some of the old
languages in his hair.
Knows without my saying
that I hurt, that all is not well.
I'm never surprised when I see him
with packages in hand, talking about
what it could and ought to be.

He's a dreamer and that is good.
Man with vision can conjure
himself into anything.
For a long time I could not see him,
maybe he didn't know himself then.
Hardened shell of the man just forming,
him riding wild horses of desire,
taming hurricanes with his touch.

Through mangosweetness of life
he carry Jahlight so high,
I can't imagine him old and bent.
He stands tall in any time. He
   knows lessons of the willow,
      knows call of the sea,
         he brother some love...

My uncle with the cooper glow,
silvered smile, chancing life
doing a fancy lindy hop, bebop step.
High southern sun, he was his mothers'
creole dream, secondborn son.
Six sisters and he, brillant,
making a mockery out of savanah wind.
He was a child of the sea, hair
full of real waves Negro men
were famous for in the 1940's.
His moustache a sly, tender
line that seduced many.

From european ports during WWII, he sent gold
covered china, silks and fine linen.
Afterwards he headed north,
bringing with him a woman named
Jewell, dark amethyst
eroding under urban squall.

Surprise knife of a killer took
him home in some back room
at the Theresa Hotel. His Jewell
would shatter into a thousand pieces
and vanish, leaving three generations
looking for any sign of woman,
mother-friend, wondering at the mystery
of that pretty man from Charleston,
doing the bugaloo with life.

Joseph Johnson

Maybe you knew before
any of us, that you were
leaving, surrendering
gemstones of your life to
death, most cunning of thiefs.
All our years of separation,
cutting the light in your eyes,
roping your mind. Your hands,
brown blackbirds carrying a
bottle of whiskey and a bible.
You, skin darkened ruby over
crease in sula's eye.
Old kongo, magic hands
fixed everything that was
broken, needy and woman.
When you could, you got up
early most mornings and
rode the "El" to work, measuring
your dreams in the light bouncing
off your black derby with the green feather.

This woman searches for you
in pictures, pieces of cloth,
old anecdotes. How I look for
you in your mother's face, but
see you in your father's omniscient
eyes. Nine times you tried for boys
reaping girlspirits, watching your six
sons become premature ash of northern dreams.
In the end, none of that mattered.
Riffs of Danny Boy filled the air as you
cut a rugged path back to the ancestors.

I sat for weeks, Holiday blue,
holding your bag with the red dice,
and old striped shirt, rummaging
for the part of you I lost. Now
I hold rubies of you life to a larger
truth, quickening my dreams onward.

Seventeen years since your death.
I try to see what there is
of you that lives in me,
beyond my humor, sweet alto singing.
More than tears, I am in
need of truth, unembittered
whole like your hands, sweet
like the love you shared with Mama.

Arcs of heartmusic coming out
a two string guitar, same way
your "Kentucky Bandoliers" always
knew how to play foostomping,
soul-go-home music strumming
through memories window.

For PG

You said, you found your
grandfather's spirit one day
in the six shadows that
surrounded you in this New World.
Long time ago, before you left that
island of burnished copper
and tamarind root, he put
his mark on you. To your
mother, a vast hurricane,
frustrating in her evilness
you were rotted piece of cassava root,
island simpleton, a nobody's nobody.
Though you were, silent solider,
eager eyes burning encouragement
to my world weary spirit.

You said, I brought your grandfather's
spirit back to you, even as you
stood "dreaded down" mopping the
floor of this backroom cafeteria.
I saw the hunger, glazed brilliance
of recognition. How you scrubbed
the floor quickly, skipping some places
so you could hear the poets' poetry.
It didn't bother you, to sit among
ladies with hair the various shades
of ocean waves. You came because
I promised what you knew,
I could not give. Your presence
became the coal covered diamonds
of dreams held to the light.

Bones bent and curled,
old man shivers in 97th
winter of his life. Inside
gentrified building, he is
the last of seven tenants.
Porcelain teeth in shallow spotted glass.
Slop jar behind the door.
Insurance policy in Bessie's
old dresser bureau. Keys to the
good book under his pillow.
Upstairs, a memory fading like
swirling sea of multi-colored leaves
that line his block. In winter, arctic winds,
see ancient spirit elder, doing
a three legged bop, over rugged ice.

We met at the junction of
street and street.
Him tall with island all over him
walking like he own the earth.
His hands take to the air like
so many promises, as he follow me
to one corner, into the store, out of
the store, onto another corner. I rest,
he talks. How he wish me long life
so he have a long, long time to love me, he say.
Inside urban mask gentle flash reveal
gap tooth, on the bottom where
I almost fall in.
He lyrics me with all that
mango and honey in his mouth.
Slight rustle of rocking hips teases
back one more shredded piece of my armor.
As he talks, I stare questions into the white
of his hair, the nape of his neck.
He doing alright, so I let him talk
match his lies with my own,
surrender only my laughter as he lay out
his plans for me. In two months, he say
in two months, I give you baby.
Maybe he can feel it, but right then and there
I plan my escape. Throw his application
in the wind, soundlessly. He know it too,
cause he change his song. He say,
"let me take you out and dance.
Let's have a good time and dance," he say.
But I'm already in the wind,
leave the mangoes and honey
down by street and street.

So many are trying to get what you
naturally carry in your mystery
Your face is a soliloquy of contrasts
so smooth, it could be a womans,
a silver hooped earring in one ear,
blunt edge of a strong jaw line.
One of your eyes black as the
African ocean watching the coming of slavers.
The other ancient and blue as Bessie Smith's lost arm.
You are centered in the battle between the two.
A sweet urgency calls out to me.
There are so few who can love both sides,
seeing you whole. Inside broken
lines of your face,
a peaceful unity exists,
intentional as your smile
and raw, unpolished gem of my desire.

Here are rivers raining
at the top of my womb
where redden apple of my need
opens and changes fast.
Underneath wet, black eyes
of a riverwoman there is all
this music more ancient and
beautiful than the white rim
of a hunger I have no name for.

I lose all my silver songs, my many
tongues reasoning in the quiet
gaze of yours eyes. I can barely
hold the flicker of you time
burning ashes smoke the ground.

Between us, there is more
than the complication of skin,
seas of spirit tendrils
with some kind of knowing I can
and cannot name. Here are rivers
sitting at the top of my womb
cataracts of lust sear my eyes
as the dreary sweat of sleeplessness
haunts me.

How is it that I have
all this fruit for you and
you are eating the backs of eggs, wicked crusts
of memories, lean veins of new loves.

UNTITLED

We love each other
to the beat
in the silence of
electronic movements
we cry laughter
into empty spaces
   of each other
      searching
         for the music.

My rootman knows which trees to pick,
which ones to leave alone.
He knows which trees make good sounds,
which ones make good canoes.
His all knowing hands can find
the ones that make cloth,
trees that could talk. Always knew
which ones healed, exactly
the ones that belong to spirits.

He can send a thought across
time, won't use a talking drum.
Can wear the whole spectrum of light
in his skin and still reflect back
one vision of truth. Will conjure
a conjure man for my dreams, change
forms, appear as flying fish.

My rootman, keeper of treestories,
ancestor secrets and the song of
ancient woodmen. Can cast wrought
iron over wooden base relief
make a Benin mask breathe,
live for centuries. Entice the white
openings in my coweries to talk all night.
Son of indigo mercy,
doing the kongo all over me.

Rancid reasoning of a thousand
hands wrap around his body.
Yellow flecks of couscous still
in the corners of his mouth.
Amaryl and the children, six
glistening black pools, his last
view of home.

The first stones miss him,
as he jerks and dances.
Sooner than he expected,
his body rings with thunder.
His life dreams roll away in
grimy, Sudan sweat of his hair.

He knows they will never hear him,
the ones that cover themselves
in black from head to foot.
His truth, spurts out in red
uneven lines, forming puddles
of disbelief at his feet.
Even the desert women hungry,
lean on hope, turn their back on him.
He surrenders heartworn
to the cool darkness,
exploding in his head.

For Jean Michel Basquiat

It is a long night, I have
to go places beyond this skin.
Basquiat eyes haunt, as I filter
through tears and the absence of sun.
In the background are sounds of paint
hitting a wet canvas. I can't
begin to understand the task of
recapturing innocence, finger painted,
graffitied scrawlings, a modern heiroglyph,
disorderly order. How in every picture
was always this lone, sad, black man who
already knew the sound of his own death.

You, the bush spirit that can only enter the village
at great risk, not because we are so afraid, but
your razor quick quick truth, cuts everything in sight.
Even your own hands bleed into the paint.
Basquiat, your people do not recognize you
nor do they call you by name.
You, who might have been Warhol's wonder boy,
know your art is a loa to another time.

Can you see the dots, hear
wails between the black holes.
All those slashed words, every red,
yellow, green pyre a painted altar. Feel
rough scratchy edge of a noose getting tighter.
Find him, find that horse with no rider.
Puerto Rican, nappy, spiraled dread, blood nail.
Over everything is the wicked sounding
of a million black men, seeking freedom.

Every sign, Samo, imprint of
brush, hand, feet lives.
While you of the swift, swift
funky,
black,
triple,
vision
never leaves.

Just this day, white winter
chill in the air soft blues,
dull amber of an early dusk.
I look up and there is Ngugi
nappy hair and all, the universe
jumping off his blackness,
Ngugi wa Thiong'o walking
into a coffee shop circa
1994, Greenwich Village.

His freedom makes the eye laugh.
Who would have thought
from the days of his Kikuyu
village, travelling upon a river
between mau mau sounds, warrior
words, tribal marks into adulthood,
that he, would be here in my world.

How did he know but for the meager
grains of wheat, kin and clan
would turn upon each other, neo
colonial style and make
the generations tremble.

During his years of protest,
banned books, forced exile
he kept his war tools poised,
writing of the missing, disappeared.
This african epic repeats
and repeats like a eddy upon river
swollen with one million bodies,
so many petals of blood.
A backward looking, stuttering

bird mocks his efforts, unable
to find reason or voice.

Here at the corner
of 8th and University,
I watch him walk
in his rapid pace,
coffee in hand.
I watch him, thankful,
the beautiful ones
are still among us.

"If a leaf falls from a tree and nobody praises it, then the leaf must praise itself."

—Nupe people, Northern Nigera

For Hannah

Is someone who knew you
before you was born.
Is someone who knows
your song before you can speak.
Was my grandma, who
in the dark years of my life,
in naive wanderings
of early footsteps
became my Carolina sun,
my we, that knew me
before I did.

Over air, over land
through muddy waters of life,
gris gris kept the pace
followed me where ever I went.

In my fourth year, when I first
walked the Carolina shore,
I imagined she looked at me
a chocolate, stringbean of a girl
with more hair and lip than I could handle
and wondered, what we gonna do with this one
as she place a bowl of okra gumbo in front of me.

Later, under quilted dreams of northstar
she told me to sleep, while cleared
an extra room for my spirit,
cause, she knew tomorrow was already
today in my life.

Under that geechee, Carolina sun
healing balm of my ancestors
danced all around me.   ˋ
I grew flourishing on
fresh fruit, song and seafood.
Still, I wanted more.

Nomadic at heart
I left, heading north
into a time that never was
but is now.

Somehow the gris gris kept the pace,
followed me wherever I went.

In the six or seven years
I lived outside of myself,
she must have known,
cause my dreams always took me home
to my geechee sun of ancestral spirits.

Some ten years later, I hurried
back to the Carolina sun.
I knew very strongly there's
more juju in the mojo than I can tell.
Under grandma's septembered lids
flickering with Mt. Pleasant memories,
time passed was lost. The future
took hold in my clearing vision.
When leaving again for my quilted northstar,
she leaned over her years and said very clearly to me,
"I'll see you again."

Nai a shimmering silvered colored lake
daytime sky, pastel blue and cloudless.
November flower on water, her leaves brilliant,
Aztec gold.

Nai song like Sonny Rollins midnight tenor sounds.
A low moan on Savannah wind flyin' north, free.

She is the color of brown burlap evenly woven.
Her black hair is tight kinky curls laughing
against the grain.

Macaw red leaf with honeyed sunbursts,
piercing her stem.
Nai taste of tamarind and coconut.

She is rounded edges of pottery smooth in age,
calm and black like the blueness of indigo.
Laughing creole in gumbo.

She is the geechee
in me.

A coconut brown man
old, gnarled with varicosities
sits stroking his granddaughter's head.
She is two maybe three,
fresh as greens in a July picking.

Eddie his friend of forty years, sits nearby,
talking like always, in the past tense.
Like the time they went fishing at midnight,
found this woman, pretty as luck
on an Indian head nickel.

Or the time they ran through
three counties trying to escape
the klan. Thought they were
blood burning moonsong,
when an empty freight train
came chugging along,
just like some old Geechee hoodoo.
Rode dam near two states away,
before they caught their breath.

Now, with oats of youth
full grown and gone,
he sits on limestone steps
looking at window boxes of Marigolds,
Zinnias and Hyacinth.

He counts time
through granddaughter's eyes.
She, color of pound cake
favors his first wife
with her little ways.

Lips poked out, hands on hips, sway backed
comely, she jumps impatiently
as his brown hands
warm her to a smile.

In shade of ancient Magnolias
I sit alone,
in a space where women go
when we can not
when we do not
want to give
or be taken for
anything or anyone.

Times like now, I simply can't and don't
want to huddle under old myths.
Ritual of scrapping peas in a circle
is lost on me,
as I know, we can barely look in each other's eyes
peacefully, and
yet, need a far
deeper healing than the
dull thud music
of shelled peas hitting a pan.

Rusted edges of old dreams fall,
blocking the path where I walk.
The call of a million Blue Sundays
follows me, scratching freedom into my palms.

I crave wisdom of my
woman waters, netting a peace
that goes past unfulfilled dreams
of women who birthed life before me.
This august time, a well worn callous I
tear at, always searching for skin of new selves.
I know in my silent spiritwringing,
laying on hands, arched back of holyghost shivers

something different,
my own, must be rendered
silvered and whole
into my life's meaning.

She had the kinda' beauty
made men crazy
other women, brown women, evil.
She had the kinda' beauty
home nurtured, simple
delicate and fragile like lace, she was
hinty colored, caramel with cream.
Josephine high kickin' legs
eternal black hair to waist.

Once she dreamed,
centered her whole world around him.
Wash him deep with her honey love,
Oshun, him down, you know.
He savored her, like a good luck penny.
She spiraled behind white picket fences, and
perfectly landscaped flowers, with no scent.

Once she dreamed to blow trombone sounds,
tap dance across the moon, wear diamonds in her nose,
eat chocolate and champagne.
She always wanted to break, stomp over
glaring eyes and staccato tongues,
let her black come down all over them.

Even the push of four children
some thirty years of him
visiting every now and again,
did not alter her beauty.
Unable to protect hallowed center of herself,
she surrendered to storm of her years.

Later, with her life circling around
whisper thin, she wore her eyes inside out.
Her beauty, she disfigured.
Behind rows, and rows of empty glasses,
she moan old catgut, wobbleknee,
brokenphoenix fire, geechee woman blues.

I remember you back
then, your 75 years to
my 12. Saturday's you
would buy 20 pounds of shrimp,
15 of fish. Together, we
would sit around the den table
scaling whiting, porgies, shark,
butter and any fish fool enough
to jump into a geechie man's net.

You would tell me stories,
pieces of your life, "man told
me once, don't fall in love with no
geechie gal, she'll hold on forever."

I learned to clean fish
by watching you open their
white bellies and push your hand in
pulling out roe and guts in one thorough swope,
blood and salt sea smell
spewing everywhere.

Your strength three generations deep
showed me how to handle life's mess.
Clean a whiting, season him, fry him
proper like any geechie girl.

In the end, the day's
catch like so many men
lay between us. We
had humbled them, laid
them bare, open, with
the truth of our hands.

Dull patina
over rim of blue eye.
Echoes of amber and grey glimmering.
Hands brown, arthritic, lively as Robins.
In her voice one hears thunder of Fannie Lou.
She 97, witty, lady of daywonder,
organizer of the organizers,
she earned her time and proud of it.
She from a place full of lemon swamp and sweet grass.
Found all my history in her smile.
She make all heavy loads lighter.

That all this has happened before,
witness purple flames of dreams gone home.
Awesome ancestral wrinkling of time.
Children grown and gone some four times over.
She sits alone against yellow southern backdrop,
listening to the furious flutter of things undone.

Undaunted, she shares her memory
some three times my life span,
making clear to me all the reasons why,
we young have to be everstrong.
Her truth, our truth,
makes all heavy loads lighter,
    all heavy loads lighter.

She was music whole note.
Was a reggae, bebop, blues
singin' woman.

She learned to sing in a place where the scent of magnolias filled
the air and hot sun danced across the nape of her bare neck. She
sang in a place where men still knew how to love women and leave
them weeping in eternal blue dawns.

She learned from an old songstress, who taught her to hold her
notes, lungs bursting, diaphragm stretching becoming a strong
flexible instrument.

Clara listened deeply for inner songs, she created color from sweet
memories. Her song became a particular place, a special mood. She
learned to sing in a circle of women who made rocks weep with their
sweetness, their song made water pure and clear form in your eyes.

She learned to sing in the woman of herself. Clara's singing was
more than a sound. Her music was like a staccato drumbeat running
up and down your spine. Her music, was like new money jingling in
your pockets, was like the sound of rolling sky. She was midnight
thunder laughing kisses over brown ears, singing.

Clara, reggae, bebop blues
singin' woman,
was music whole note,
melody and lyric in one.

BAHIA NOTES

I am caught in the roar of the ocean
mad movement of eddies and waves
make patchwork designs with moonlight.
Waves rise,
salt sea air
dances on my skin.
It is here that I come
to find the muse,
listen to the call of Yemanja,
song of my own voice
blending into a night four hundred years long.

> I imagine an overburden ship
> her cargo, a people this land
> has never seen before.
> Storm ridden night,
> evil and dark as eternity.
> Moon heavy and weeping.
> Windy brake between land and
> sea is where I notice
> coming of first blacks.
> Their weakened limbs trembling,
> darting eyes take in the scarred,
> reddened face of the daughter, Bahia
> so much like home, but different.

In the first breaths of dawn
I surrender to the mystical sight
of the Bay of Saints.
A thousand drums beating,
agogo bells ringing.
I capture time,
cross turquoise waters,

jump spirit bridges to see,
remember their fury, and songs.
Palmeres blue, Angolan moan
still flow in my blood,
as I walk on the land of the daughter.

Nana Vasconcelos

My heart, listen
I am unable to go and say
I do not have the words to sing
but see if you will, what I hear.

In the time before the dark,
it was known that all musicians
were spirit, were teachers
Music was the essence, way back
key to it all.

The sky, she is dressed in night,
a half-moon embraces her.
Scented wind flies through
a mosaic of trees, fireflies
and the slippery laughter of
children playing.

In the midst of it all, stands
Nana, berimbau man.
Gourdspeaker, drumtalker, timbale spirit,
keeper of African night sounds.
Spirit of bahian earth music,
taking me somewhere over water, over earth,
going past time and space.
Reclaiming the sound of the African sea,
song of nightwinds whirling,
call of the orishas,
bassdrum moans of lovers, loving
and me, on a lone string across
a music laden gourd. . .

My heart, listen,
I am unable to go and say.
Speak if you will, for both of us.

I eat blue sky blue of Bahia
every morning
sun opens my skin
to the bone,
it's all the freedom I know.

Her face a searing sea of questions,
she cooks rice and stewed fish for her guests.
Even as we sit, a green coolness on my neck,
I know she is first wife.

It's in the sagging slope
of rounded shoulders,
worn hands on hips.
In the space under dark circled eyes,
the way her whole body
shouts how tired she is.
Her sons, her man
the terriro are her universe.

She is a young woman, but old.
Lines across her forehead, tell me, she has
long said goodbye to romance, to love.
When he brings home a new wife,
she fights the air and looks the other way.
Her anger something ancient and remote.
That makes her old, too old.

We form an uneven circle in this
lightless pink and green house
hewed out of the side of a hill.
I bite down on the simple bitterness
of dreams gone awry, the pain of it all
coats my tongue, wearily.
I am sad for her and yet,
afraid of her vengeance.

Caporiestas dance in la Marqueta Modelo square,
gourded sound of the berimbau,
drums sounding.
Singers spice my ears in Yoruba and Afro-Portuguese.
Coconut milk and palm oil in all my food.
The smell and taste of Angola,
salted wind on my lips my thighs.
This anago man
gives me his eye,
Bahia nightblack eye.
I samba in his trembling,
he pulls me across time.
Eats the poetry of my mouth whole.
We fly past language and gather
like tendrils of spirit.
Aboriginal reddened locks,
warm my back.
Under narrowed waist, lean and muscular
I reveal all the dances I've ever known.
We lay clean and free
as the yellow fruit of his terriro.
This Anago man
gives me his eye,
Bahia nightblack
spirit eye.

A KNOWING

"I see the coming of the long green rain"
—Henry Dumas

I gather the calm of yesterdays wishes,
over burning fields of truth
I hold in my hand, my heart
dreams, visionsong.
Through broken bits of mirror, glass,
elusive flutter of fins,
between wet suck of thighs,
I carry my dream children.

Though I turn into tree, then song,
under blackened earth
they find my name and others of my clan.
Way underneath the rocks, green shoots grow.
They burst through my blindness,
feed at the long fruit of my thoughts.
I ride purple nightwinds alone,
bank smooth stones along the footpath to my soul.
In the eye of storm they find shelter,
ancient spider strength
in the winding clover of my lies.
A riotous lust assaults the senses,
misted perfume of the spirits.

Respectfully, tenderly, I carry
flame of their lives desire on my head.
Gris gris gather under shining waterfall of my eyes.
I givein to the broken clay of my hands
moving deeper into the wide ark of truth.

For Aminata Moseka/Abbey Lincoln

Sound of thunder in her voice,
she reaches back deep into herself.
Eyes, brilliant coals
trust no one.
Private rivers
flow across, down
sides of her face,
sparking the fired
spirit to life.
See line woman, song-singing
her way from field hollers
to black classical music
haves her way with us.
We are taken in
underneath the web of skin
near hollows of her ribbed soul eyes
where the heart sings, weary
but free....

It is looking at you
in the center of life.
Dreads thick as your dreams.
Your spirit ready,
homeward bound.
Face full, lined, yet
transcendent. Your body with
out breasts, without womb,
is fat and fertile
with your own life.
It is here, looking
upon your face
in the sweetness of life
that the tears come.

Knowing your words,
soundings, you,
who hold no squint eye
to death, stand ready, yet
still dancing your power woman
dance, holding council between
the worlds. You of the long,
long faith, keeper of woman word power.
More than the fury of your womb,
the sleek long seeds of your thoughts
catch and keep life, flower
and reflower, pressing your
daughters, sisters, mothers
to be more than the thread
the weaver, weaves, to be more
like warriors and lovers, fiercely
owning self, life, wealthy
in their womaness.

It happens sometimes when walking down the street, standing on a subway platform, sitting at a bar. I look up from a preoccupied calm into a face, into a pair of eyes that force me to stop, the unfamiliar becoming a flash of lightning across a lake. Perhaps it's his particular shade of berried blue blackness that strikes me, that calls me, all that beauty with the sun underneath, just humming.

More than that, it's the feeling that fills my chest that tells me, I know this person, although it was another place, some other time. We lock eyes, holding in two megaseconds all the stories of our past. We can't speak, our voices are gone. So we stare at each other knowingly, almost lost with the mystery of where do I know you from.

Our western tribal scars torn over memories. How many times did a man, a woman, a child in slavery times walk away to get some water, some wood and just never came back? How many times did a man, a woman set up house, make children, only to have them sold off, never to see each other again.

In moments like these when there are no words to speak that carry though time, this momentary reconnection of a broken past makes me ache with remembrance. It makes me long for a time before chains, when we were all knowing, before our bond, our primal love for each other was broken. Now, we stand staring questions over memories we no longer have access to and just for a second, we glimpse at the face, the collective spirit of all the people we have been.

I look away, the train is coming, the drink just arrive and forcibly I resign our past out of reach. I stretch a hand forward realizing that we have to take a different road home, live among different people, speak other tongues, worship different spirits and save whatever we can, as we move on.

Do you think that when they built this place,
they really had us in mind. Could you see back
to 1902. If I had lived here, it would only be
to cook, clean or wetnurse some other womans' child.
Do you think any black woman ever poeted
across a golf course? It's something that
sinks in the skin of mystery unveiled, like how
all that copper came out of the womb of Azania, and Latin
America. Did they stop to recognize the sanctity
of any Mayan, Indian people. It's such a short walk
from Iroquois to Maya, to Azania, you know.
Can you smell the stink in the wind when the muse
refuses to pick up her lyre and sing here.
What artists came here during that time? Were they
a mild extravagance, not to be taken seriously
but tolerated. Do you really think they had us in
mind when they built this place. It's how the captain's
eyes only meet mine inside a tall tale. Can you imagine
ten years work to dredge an island for whom? How many died
on the way? How many are in the mists, thicket of the trees?
What do I say, standing on the land of one who made his
living out of the eyes and souls of my people, death money.
What do I say to my family in Azania, in Zaire, in Brooklyn?
Shall I ransom my thoughts, prostitute my history,
line my throat with so much copper. Do you really think
they had us in mind when they built this place?

Used to be,
we threw our different ones
into the bush
at birth, giving them back
to what evil created them.
Even sold them to slavers.
Their death price, their life price
a purification of the tribe.

In other places, we used to
show our different ones
how to find God's gift in them.
Make ways for them to be here with pride
whole lives, living full of us.
We used to know secrets
of the god of the white cloth,
make a one legged man dance,
turn a pimp into a revolutionary,
a poet into the north star.

Nowadays, with our different ones,
those women with too many
women friends, that man
down the street with that
four letter disease and
that woman wearing the hefty
plastic bag, fighting on any corner
with her ghosts, we wrap
them in an abysmal silence.
Force fit a shimmering blindness
around our collective eye.
The fittest becoming the unfit.

Do we throw them away
into the grey, urban, concrete bush?
Buy back their pain with nickels
loose change, their death
a purification of the tribe?

Long before the official declaration
of war, these women, they come
bellies high with life,
draped in black from head to foot.
I barely see their faces
as they stand in my Brooklyn
living room, holding a
global dirge, collective wringing of hands.
Could be my grandmother, might
be my sister, these Iraqi, Somalian,
muslim flowers all pressed into one corner
where no perfume permeates.
Already, I know we
will kill their sons
still wet from the warmth
of their wombs. Their husbands,
brothers forced into an unholy jihad.
In this white mystical morning, we women
stand in clusters, silent for a moment.
All those burning missiles, phallacies
of war, piercing an unwelcoming earth.
Oil fields explode, blackened nova
line lungs of all human, plant and sea life.
These women stand, their black cloth,
billowing scythes, darkened clouds,
challenge me to listen.
All these pregnant comrades
holy and wailing, bearing down
on a truth none of us can hide.
As quickly as they come, they leave.
Blood of their telling thickens at my feet.

We furthest away from our African mother
seek out everything, Mali basket,
anago bead, yam dance and
coweried half-shell shields.
We wear young skin of new selves,
old ancients masked in new world ways.
Sometimes we recognize how we did survive,
claiming everything, Navajo stone, Arawak corn,
Hopi rain. African and Indian becoming
resistant, soulminds, nimble
in their splendor.

Even if now we are Bantu,
Malian, Ethiopian, Geechee,
African people, forced blend
of congoblue, copper and raffia brown,
our differences are our blessings.
Even though, there was no way
to tell which of our broken limbs
belonged to whom, we have a knowing
about who we are. We carry
an African mother's wisdom
wealthy in our knowingness.
Our differences are our blessings.

I.

Just think, all those tongues
all those people,
caught in the quickening wind.
Hinduspeak, arawakcry, african
bluesong, hopi wail,
can you see the spirits caught
in babel's confused tower.
Last night, I dreamed it was
standing upright. There is
this baby sitting on my knee,
I am in the center of a village. I own
its past and its future. Sometimes, I
paint the generations with my hands.

II.

I am in search of my
mother tongue,
I am in search of the
mother tongue.
American can't hold me,
has always been my second language,
I am, in search. I seek my mother tongue.
More than the sounding of women
it is an understanding,
a knowing about cosmos,
this universe of all our bodies,
earth.

Just last night I was in
search of the mother tongue,

found myself in the bush
of Ruwanda, listening to
wailing mother spirits, knowing
in the African cosmos, one million
everyday people, like me, like
you just died from military bullets.

III.

Last night, I dreamed all
the leaning faiths, all
the leaning truths everywhere
were standing upright.
I can see it in the smoke of Sarajevo,
how the whole city weeps. What happened
when they pulled the wall down,
what happened when they undid the
boundaries. This new Europe bleeds
like in the old days, see the same
blood filled river, flowing through Haiti.

IV.

I wonder, if Lloyd McNeil remembers when
music was waiting to happen in him,
waiting for him to discover, metaphor,
paint and half notes, his
mind a fertile rooster, flying free.
Ten years ago, Walcott said,
surrender and I did, and from that
moment, that forever, the sound
of poetry has been calling ever since.

V.

Mind of my mind,
practicing guerilla warfare.
Mind of my mind
growing flowers in heart of
the Stuy. Where does a woman
go for solitude, can't find
Sarton's garden anywhere. Picking glass,
cigarette butts, dog doo, condoms,
and candy wrappers from the earth,
a woman too, you know.
All she wants is our respect,
all we want is our respect.

VI.

Just this morning, I remembered my
awakeness, saw the possibilities
of flowers that couldn't find the sun.
Heard the babel in my neighborhood go
from confusion to clarity. Saw this
artist who refused government aid, refused
to be a state artist, found a way,
made a way to keep wild poppies of her art
alive. She knows freedom doesn't require
an application, just pursuit.

VII.

Last night, I dreamed
all those made to lean generations,
all the leaning flags, leaning
people of Africa, were
standing upright.

Tryptch—Part III

By this river, see my face
ancient marks etched in the
cheek of my thoughts, old lappas,
emotions envy at my feet. New
world now, I gather wealth
with my smile.
Sing only when I want to.

Page 55 — Sister Sukie II
Akuabana: Ashanti doll of fertility and healing

Page 27 — The Delta
Erzulie: Voudoun river and love deity
Oshun: Yoruba love and river deity

Page 59 — Medicine Men
Ashe: the power to make things happen

Page 62 — Bloodknot
Kentucky Bandoliers: One of the first all boys bands in Charleston,
S.C.

Page 79 — What Keeps Us Alive
gris-gris: an African magical charm

Page 84 — Geechie Woman
Blue Sunday was invoked during slavery times when black women
wanted to birth free children.

Page 886 — Ayana's Blues
Oshun: Yoruba love and river deity

Page 89 — Sister Maime Fields
Author of *Lemon Swamp and Other Places*

Page 99 — Saudades
Saudades: Longings

JACQUELINE JOHNSON

Jacqueline Johnson was born in Philadelphia. A graduate of New York University, she is presently working on a Masters degree in creative writing at the City College of New York. She has received writing fellowships from the Blue Mountain Center and the MacDowell Colony and has been a New York Foundation for the Arts Gregory Millard Fellow in Poetry. She won the 1987 poetry award given by Mid-Atlantic Writers Association of Baltimore, Maryland. She is also the author of *Stokely Carmichael: Leaders in the Civil Rights Movement*, which was published in 1990 by Silver Burdett Books, an imprint of Simon & Shuster, and contributed to *UpSouth: African American Migration* (New Press, 1994) and *Streetlights: Illuminating Black Urban Tales* (Penguin Books, 1996). She lives in Brooklyn, New York.

THE WHITE PINE PRESS POETRY PRIZE

The annual White Pine Press Poetry Prize, established in 1995, offers a cash award of $500 plus publication of the winning manuscript. Manuscripts are accepted between July 15 and October 15 each year, and the winning manuscript is published the following spring. Please write for additional details.

1995   *Zoo & Cathedral* by Nancy Johnson
        Selected by David St. John

1996   *Bodily Course* by Deborah Gorlin
        Selected by Mekeel McBride

1997   A *Gathering of Mother Tongues* by Jacqueline Joan Johnson
        Selected by Maurice Kenny

These books are available in fine bookstores
or from
White Pine Press, 10 Village Square, Fredonia, New York 14063
Telephone: 716/672-5743

AMERICAN POETRY FROM WHITE PINE PRESS

BODILY COURSE
Deborah Gorlin
90 pages $12.00 paper
Winner 1996 White Pine Press Poetry Prize

TREEHOUSE: NEW & SELECTED POEMS
William Kloefkorn
224 pages $15.00 paper

CERTAINTY
David Romtvedt
96 pages $12.00 paper

ZOO & CATHEDRAL
Nancy Johnson
80 pages $12.00 paper
Winner 1995 White Pine Press Poetry Prize

DESTINATION ZERO
Sam Hamill
184 pages $15.00 paper
184 pages $25.00 cloth

CLANS OF MANY NATIONS
Peter Blue Cloud
128 pages $14.00 paper

HEARTBEAT GEOGRAPHY
John Brandi
256 pages $15.00 paper

LEAVING EGYPT
Gene Zeiger
80 pages $12.00 paper

WATCH FIRE
Christopher Merrill
192 pages $14.00 paper

BETWEEN TWO RIVERS
Maurice Kenny
168 pages $12.00 paper

TEKONWATONTI: MOLLY BRANT
Maurice Kenny
209 pages $12.00 paper

DRINKING THE TIN CUP DRY
William Kloefkorn
87 pages $8.00 paper

GOING OUT, COMING BACK
William Kloefkorn
96 pages $11.00 paper

JUMPING OUT OF BED
Robert Bly
48 pages $7.00 paper

WHY NOT
Joel Oppenheimer
46 pages $7.00 paper

TWO CITIZENS
James Wright
48 pages $8.00 paper

SLEEK FOR THE LONG FLIGHT
William Matthews
80 pages $8.00 paper

WHY I CAME TO JUDEVINE
David Budbill
72 pages $7.00 paper

AZUBAH NYE
Lyle Glazier
56 pages $7.00 paper

SMELL OF EARTH AND CLAY
East Greenland Eskimo Songs
38 pages $5.00 paper

FINE CHINA: TWENTY YEARS OF EARTH'S DAUGHTERS
230 pages $14.00 paper

POETRY IN TRANSLATION FROM WHITE PINE PRESS

THE FOUR QUESTIONS OF MELANCHOLY
Tomaz Salamun
224 pages $15.00

THESE ARE NOT SWEET GIRLS
An Anthology of Poetry by Latin American Women
320 pages $17.00

A GABRIELA MISTRAL READER
232 pages $15.00

ALFONSINA STORNI: SELECTED POEMS
72 pages $8.00

CIRCLES OF MADNESS: MOTHERS OF THE PLAZA DE MAYO
Marjorie Agosín
128 pages $13.00   Bilingual

SARGASSO
Marjorie Agosín
92 pages $12.00   Bilingual

MAREMOTO/SEAQUAKE
Pablo Neruda
64 pages $9.00   Bilingual

THE STONES OF CHILE
Pablo Neruda
98 pages $10.00   Bilingual

VERTICAL POETRY: RECENT POEMS BY ROBERTO JUARROZ
118 pages $11.00   Bilingual

LIGHT AND SHADOWS
Juan Ramon Jimenez
70 pages $9.00

ELEMENTAL POEMS
Tommy Olofsson
70 pages $9.00

FOUR SWEDISH POETS:
STROM, ESPMARK, TRANSTROMER, SJOGREN
131 pages $9.00

NIGHT OPEN
Rolf Jacobsen
221 pages $15.00

SELECTED POEMS OF OLAV HAUGE
92 pages $9.00

TANGLED HAIR
Love Poems of Yosano Akiko
48 pages $7.50 paper   Illustrated

A DRIFTING BOAT
An Anthology of Chinese Zen Poetry
200 pages $15.00

BETWEEN THE FLOATING MIST
Poems of Ryokan
88 pages $12.00

WINE OF ENDLESS LIFE
Taoist Drinking Songs
60 pages $9.00

TANTRIC POETRY OF KUKAI
80 pages $7.00

ABOUT WHITE PINE PRESS

White Pine Press is a non-profit publishing house dedicated to enriching our literary heritage; promoting cultural awareness, understanding, and respect; and, through literature, addressing social and human rights issues. This mission is accomplished by discovering, producing, and marketing to a diverse circle of readers exceptional works of poetry, fiction, non-fiction, and literature in translation from around the world. Through White Pine Press, authors' voices reach out across cultural, ethnic, and gender boundaries to educate and to entertain.

To insure that these voices are heard as widely as possible, White Pine Press arranges author reading tours and speaking engagements at various colleges, universities, organizations, and bookstores throughout the country. White Pine Press works with colleges and public schools to enrich curricula and promotes discussion in the media. Through these efforts, literature extends beyond the books to make a difference in a rapidly changing world.

As a non-profit organization, White Pine Press depends on support from individuals, foundations, and government agencies to bring you this literature that matters—work that might not be published by profit-driven publishing houses. Our grateful thanks to the many individuals who support this effort as Friends of White Pine Press and to the following organizations: Amter Foundation, Ford Foundation, Korean Culture and Arts Foundation, Lannan Foundation, Lila Wallace-Reader's Digest Fund, Margaret L. Wendt Foundation, Mellon Foundation, National Endowment for the Arts, New York State Council on the Arts, Trubar Foundation, Witter Bynner Foundation, the Slovenian Ministry of Culture, The U.S.-Mexico Fund for Culture, and Wellesley College.

Please support White Pine Press' efforts to present voices that promote cultural awareness and increase understanding and respect among diverse populations of the world. Tax-deductible donations can be made to:

White Pine Press
10 Village Square • Fredonia, NY 14063